Faith and Freedom:

The National Monument to the Forefathers

Dave Pelland

DEDICATION

To my family and friends.

CONTENTS

"No victory has ever been so pregnant in its consequences; no event in human story, save that which occurred at Bethlehem, has produced so vast a revolution in the destinies of the human race, as the immigration of the pilgrims of the Mayflower. It is worthy then of a nation's self-denial, were it necessary, to erect a memorial of gratitude, which shall embody in its design the leading characteristics of the Pilgrim mind."

—Richard Warren, president of the Pilgrim Society

INTRODUCTION

"A people capable of greatness will not forget the virtues of their fathers; reverently will they cherish them, and gratefully present them in all their luster for the respect and imitation of after ages."

—Hon. John T. Heard, the Grand Master Mason who laid the cornerstone of the Forefathers' Monument

Standing on one of the highest hills in Plymouth, Massachusetts, the National Monument to the Forefathers was dedicated upon its completion in 1889 to honor the religious pilgrims who helped to settle land that would become the United States.

The monument also honors the core values — faith, morality, trust in law, education, and liberty — that would guide the settlers as they established their community.

Although partially hidden by Plymouth's modern development and often overlooked by visitors interested in seeing the Plymouth Rock or the Mayflower replica, the Monument to the Forefathers provides an impressive tribute to those settlers, and to the beliefs that inspired their journey across the ocean and provided a foundation for the society they created in the New World.

THE PILGRIMS' JOURNEY

The Pilgrims' long journey to the shores of Plymouth started with a desire to escape religious and social persecution in their native England.

Part of a movement known as the Separatists, because they wanted to escape the pressures of the Anglican Church, the Pilgrims left Scrooby, England, for the Netherlands. After living briefly in Amsterdam, they settled in Leiden, Holland, in 1609.

Although they found religious freedom in the Netherlands, they found the adjustment challenging. Few spoke Dutch, and their largely rural background made earning a living difficult in the industrial city of Leiden. And as they settled into life in Holland, the Pilgrims became concerned their children were assimilating the Dutch culture and its social mores.

Seeking to preserve their heritage and customs, the Pilgrims sought the financial assistance of English investors to create a colony in the New World.

In September of 1620, a group of 102 Pilgrims and 30 crew members sailed from Southampton, England, aboard the leased ship Mayflower. The trip started smoothly, but they were forced to repair one of the ship's main beams more than halfway across the ocean.

The group sighted Cape Cod in November of 1620, after 65 miserable days in the cramped Mayflower. They tried to continue to the mouth of the Hudson River (today's New York City), but challenging currents prompted the group to anchor in Provincetown Harbor on November 11.

After exploring the Cape Cod coast and skirmishing with Native Americans near Eastham, Massachusetts, the Pilgrims landed in Plymouth on December 21, 1620, and surveyed the area they would settle.

THE LANDING OF THE PILGRIMS AT PLYMOUTH, MASS. DEC. 22ND 1620.

The land had been the site of a former Indian village known as Patuxet until a plague killed most of the natives about three years before the Pilgrims' arrival. The land offered several advantages to the new settlers — it had been cleared, had access to fresh water and was flanked by two large hills that offered defensive positions.

The Pilgrims began building a meeting house and homes at the start of what would be a very rough winter. Illness, food shortages and the harsh weather claimed the lives of nearly half of the settlers, and by the end of March of 1620, only 47 survivors remained.

Early the next year, the Pilgrims established a trade and mutual protection treaty with Chief Massasoit of the Wampanoag nation.

In November of 1621, about 53 Pilgrims and 90 Wampanoags came together for an after-harvest feast that provided the basis for today's traditional Thanksgiving celebration.

As more settlers arrived, the population of the Plymouth colony began to grow. In 1623, it reached

180 Pilgrims, and by 1630, Plymouth included nearly 300 settlers.

From that humble beginning, comforted by their faith and shared approach to government, the Pilgrims had established a foothold in the New World.

The Mayflower Compact

The Pilgrims began building their democratic society even before coming ashore. After anchoring in Provincetown Harbor in November of 1620, the heads of the various Pilgrim families met in the Mayflower's cabin and outlined a social framework by which they would govern the colony they were about to form.

Known as the Mayflower Compact, the agreement called for the Pilgrims to come together under a "civil body politic" that would be governed by "just and equal laws, ordinances, actives, constitutions and offices, from time to time, as shall be thought most...convenient for the general good of the colony; under which we promise all due submission and obedience."

The compact was described in 1802 by John Quincy Adams as the first "instance in human history of that positive social compact which speculative philosophers have imagined as the only legitimate source of government. Here was an unanimous and personal assent by all the individuals of the community, to the association by which they became a nation."

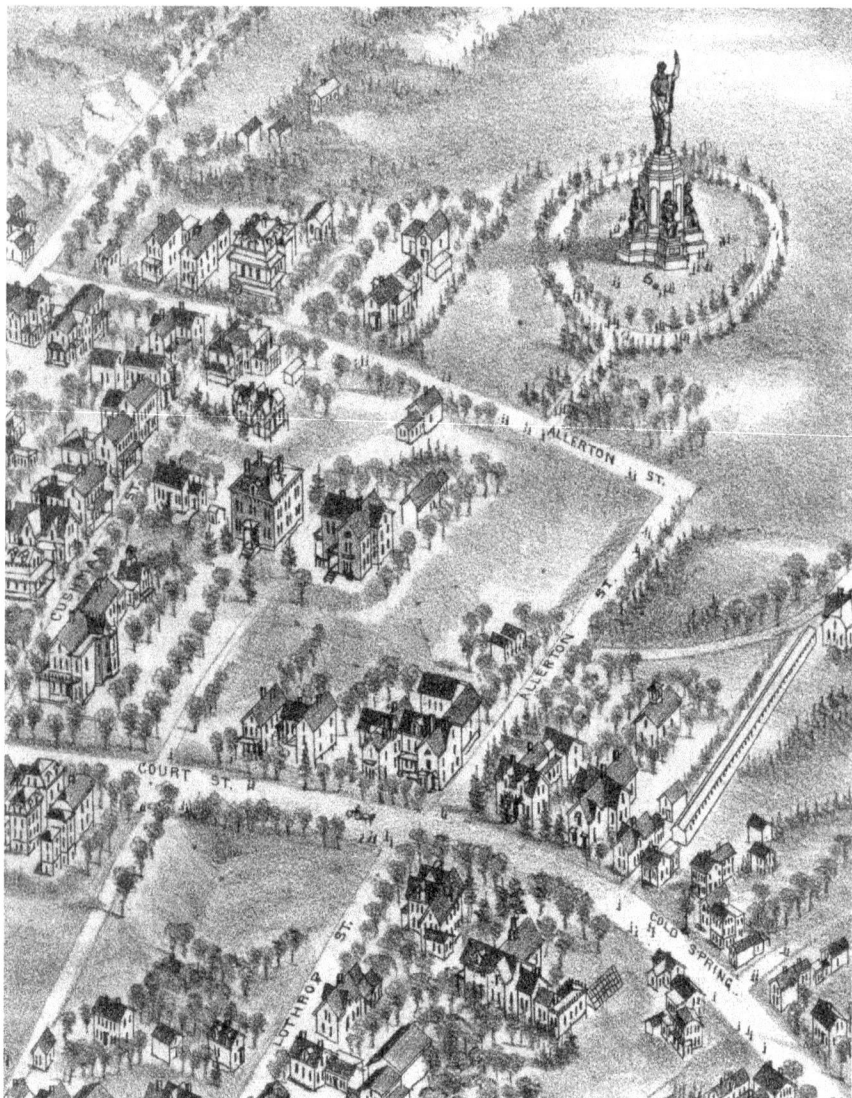

The Allerton Street site of the Forefathers Monument. Detail from an 1882 map of Plymouth.

THE MONUMENT'S LOCATION

The National Monument to the Forefathers is the dominant feature of a nearly 11-acre state park on Allerton Street, a residential neighborhood in Plymouth. The monument, which faces Plymouth Harbor and the Atlantic Ocean, originally provided a view of the harbor that has largely been obscured by trees over the years.

At 81 feet high, the monument is often described as the largest solid granite monument in the world. The statue of Faith is 36 feet high, and the monument's octagonal base is 45 feet high.

The four figures surrounding Faith commemorate the ideals — morality, law, education and liberty — upon which the Pilgrims based the new society.

The monument's base also includes four marble panels, about 80 inches long by 41 inches high, that are set in a recess in the stone base directly under the secondary figures. The bas-relief plaques depict important scenes in the Pilgrim's history, including their departure from Holland, the signing of the Mayflower Compact, their landing at Plymouth, and the signing of a treaty with Native Americans.

Unfortunately, the marble used to create the panels hasn't held up as well over the years as the granite figures have. Wind, rain and salt have caused deterioration of the marble figures, and resulted in a condition known as "sugaring" (the weathering away of crystals at the stone surface).

The monument bears a dedication on its northeast face reading, "National Monument to the Forefathers. Erected by a grateful people in remembrance of their labors, sacrifices and sufferings for the cause of civil and religious liberty."

The monument and the site were owned and maintained by the Pilgrim Society until 2001, when it was deeded to the Commonwealth of Massachusetts. Now the site of a state park, the commonwealth has completed a variety of improvements to improve visitors' experience and better reflect the importance and dignity of this magnificent monument.

Repairs to cracks in the monument are ongoing, for example, and a large bird nest atop Faith's crown has been removed in recent years. Excess brush along the edges of the site has been trimmed, improving the site's overall appearance and dignity.

The monument's historic importance has long been recognized, and the monument was listed on the National Register of Historic Places in 1974.

FAITH

The largest and most prominent figure on the monument, the Faith figure reflects the central importance of religious freedom in inspiring the Pilgrims' departure from Holland and immigration to Massachusetts.

The Faith figure is 36 feet high, and stands with her left foot on Plymouth Rock. Faith holds a Bible in her left hand, and her right hand is pointed toward the heavens, reflecting the importance of divine inspiration to guide the Forefathers to Plymouth.

Faith gazes to the east, looking toward Plymouth Harbor and symbolically toward England and Holland. The view to the east has largely been obscured by trees that have been allowed to grow in recent years.

The Faith statue was ordered in 1875 from the Hallowell Granite Company of Hallowell, Maine. Faith was completed and installed atop the National Monument on August 9, 1877.

The Faith statue is composed of 14 stones weighing

a total of 180 tons, and Faith's pedestal is 45 feet high.

Faith was funded through a donation by Oliver Ames, a Plymouth native who made a fortune as a part owner of Ames Manufacturing. The company has made shovels, picks and other implements since before the American Revolution, and earned large profits during the California gold rush and the Civil War. Oliver Ames also served as president of the Union Pacific Railroad and, along with his brother Oakes, arranged financing for the railroad's construction.

MORALITY

The Morality figure, at the base's north edge, is about 15 feet high and was installed on August 5, 1878.

Morality cradles the 10 Commandments in her left hand, and has the scroll of Revelations resting in her lap. Niches at Morality's base illustrate a Prophet and an Evangelist.

The symbolic necklace perhaps represents the 12 tribes, with whom the Pilgrims would have had a spiritual connection and a shared desire for freedom.

The figure is the work of noted sculptor Carl Conrads, and the cost was borne by the state of Connecticut as a gift to her neighbor to the north.

DEPARTURE FROM DELFT HAVEN PANEL

The panel on the face of Morality's base depicts the Pilgrims' departure from the Netherlands, their home for 11 years after fleeing persecution in their native England.

The panel, also designed by Carl Conrads, was prepared by the New England Granite Company of Hartford, Connecticut. New England Granite was one of the largest suppliers of Civil War monuments, and the firm prepared monuments not only throughout Connecticut, but also the national cemeteries at the Gettysburg and Antietam battlefields.

Recent restoration efforts have removed a considerable amount of dirt from the panel and improved its appearance, although a few cracks remain in the panel's surface.

The panel was a gift from the State of Connecticut.

LAW

The figure depicting Law was installed in November 1888, and was the final figure added to the monument's base. Law is depicted in a seated position, with two tablets cradled in his left arm.

Four fingers of the figure's right hand have been broken off, presumably by vandals.

The Law and Liberty statues, and the accompanying panels, were designed by J.H. Mahoney, a sculptor employed by the Hallowell Granite Company.

Smaller figures representing Justice and Mercy have been installed in niches flanking Law's base.

THE TREATY WITH MASSASOIT PANEL

The panel on the face of the Law statue's base represents the peace treaty between the Pilgrims and Massasoit, the leader of the native Wampanoag tribe. The Pilgrims and the Wampanoag agreed not to harm each other, to defend each other against common foes, and to trade without displaying weapons.

EDUCATION

The figure of Education depicts a seated woman, her head adored with olive branches, clutching books in her left arm. Education was very important to the Pilgrims, and later settlers, who believed in the importance of passing down moral and other responsibilities to their children.

The idea of sharing the value of education among the generations is depicted by the figures in Education's niches, who represent Wisdom and Youth.

The statue representing Education, and the panel illustrating the signing of the Mayflower Compact, were designed by sculptor Alexander Doyle of New York. Hallowell Granite completed Education and the panel.

Funds for the figure and panel were donated by Hartford lawyer and banker Roland Mather.

The figure and panel were dedicated on October 7, 1881.

SIGNING THE MAYFLOWER COMPACT

The scene depicting the signing of the Mayflower Compact sits in the base under Education, at the monument's south face.

The panel has suffered from considerable erosion and sugaring over the years.

The panel is the work of sculptor John Moffitt of New York, and was installed by the Hallowell Granite Company.

LIBERTY

The Liberty statue, at the monument's east face, was installed in November of 1888. Liberty is depicted as a seated warrior, symbolizing the struggles for freedom and liberty waged in the early years of the colony and the young United States. Liberty cradles a sword in his right arm and broken shackles in his left.

Like the Law statue on the monument's west face, the Liberty statue (and the accompanying panel) was designed by J.H. Mahoney, a sculptor employed by the Hallowell Granite Company.

The niches surrounding Liberty's base have figures depicting Peace and Tyranny.

THE PILGRIMS' LANDING

The panel on the face of Liberty's base depicts the Pilgrims' arrival in Plymouth on December 21, 1620. A forefather is being helped ashore onto the boulder that would later be known as Plymouth Rock while several of his fellow settlers wait.

The scene, by sculptor J.H. Mahoney, shows extensive wear and "sugaring" that, unfortunately, has worn away several of the settlers' facial details.

OTHER PANELS

The sides of the pedestal supporting the Faith statue have four upright panels, two of which (on the northwest and southeast sides) list the Mayflower passengers.

The northeast panel bears the dedication, and a panel on the monument's southwest face bears a quote from William Bradford, the second governor of the Plymouth colony, reading:

"Thus out of small beginnings greater things have been produced by His hand that made all things that are; and as one small candle may light a thousand, so the light here kindled hath shone unto many, yea in some sort to our whole nation; let the glorious name of Jehovah have all the praise."

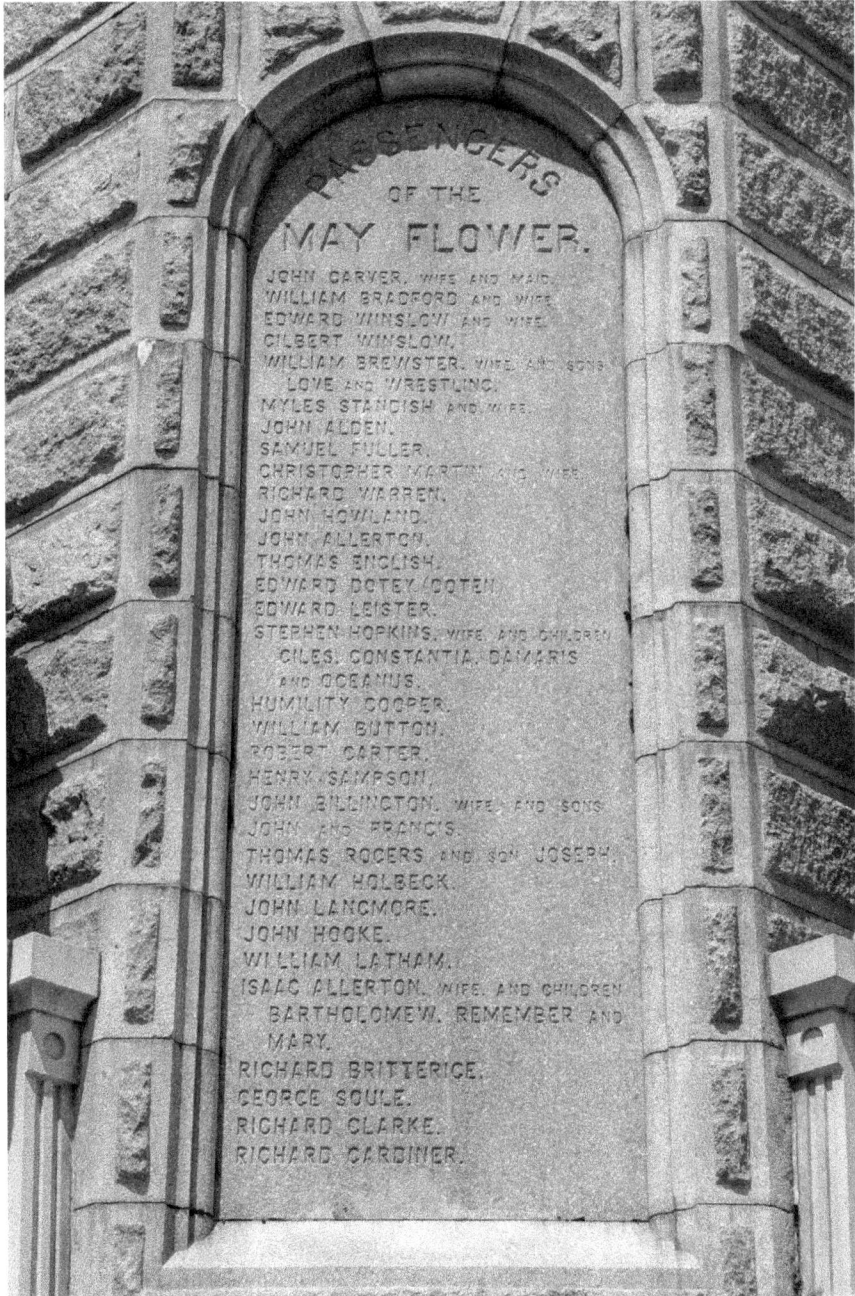

PASSENGERS
OF THE
MAY FLOWER.

JOHN CARVER, WIFE AND MAID.
WILLIAM BRADFORD AND WIFE
EDWARD WINSLOW AND WIFE.
GILBERT WINSLOW.
WILLIAM BREWSTER. WIFE AND SONS
LOVE AND WRESTLING.
MYLES STANDISH AND WIFE.
JOHN ALDEN.
SAMUEL FULLER.
CHRISTOPHER MARTIN AND WIFE.
RICHARD WARREN.
JOHN HOWLAND.
JOHN ALLERTON.
THOMAS ENGLISH.
EDWARD DOTEY (DOTEN)
EDWARD LEISTER.
STEPHEN HOPKINS. WIFE AND CHILDREN
GILES. CONSTANTIA. DAMARIS
AND OCEANUS.
HUMILITY COOPER.
WILLIAM BUTTON.
ROBERT CARTER.
HENRY SAMPSON.
JOHN BILLINGTON. WIFE AND SONS
JOHN AND FRANCIS.
THOMAS ROGERS AND SON JOSEPH.
WILLIAM HOLBECK.
JOHN LANGMORE.
JOHN HOOKE.
WILLIAM LATHAM.
ISAAC ALLERTON. WIFE AND CHILDREN
BARTHOLOMEW. REMEMBER AND
MARY.
RICHARD BRITTERIGE.
GEORGE SOULE.
RICHARD CLARKE.
RICHARD GARDINER.

OTHER SITE FEATURES

While visitors to the National Monument to the Forefathers are likely to be impressed by the monument's scale, there are a number of other interesting features in the small park surrounding the monument.

The pedestrian pathways leading to the monument are decorated with four large granite scallop shells that originally decorated the granite canopy over Plymouth Rock (which was replaced by the current portico in 1921). Each shell is 2.5 feet high.

The former Plymouth Rock canopy also provided two granite bollards, located along the foot of the path to Liberty, that were topped with pyramids. The bollards were installed on the site between 1920 and 1935.

There are also granite bollards at the foot of the sidewalks on each side of the vehicle entrance. About 2.5 feet tall, they have rectangular bases and quarter-round tops. In photographs before the 1920s, four bollards can be seen at the corners where the paths toward Liberty and Morality met the circular drive. The fate of the other two bollards isn't known.

The site has two granite platforms, located north and south of the monument, just beyond the paved circular area at the base of the monument. Roughly 5.5 feet by 6.5 feet, the platforms have attachment holes that were probably used for view scopes in the mid-20th century.

Several cut granite stones sit on the site: Two near the vehicle entry, and 14 on the southwestern edge of the circular drive. The stones may be from the original Plymouth Rock canopy.

A small restroom building near the monument is not open, but may be repaired in the future.

PLANNING THE MONUMENT

Planning for ways to honor the Forefathers began in the early part of the 19th Century. The Pilgrim Society was founded in 1820 to commemorate the 200th anniversary of the Pilgrims' landing in Plymouth, and to procure "a suitable lot or piece of ground for the erection of a monument to perpetuate the memory of the virtues, the enterprise and the unparalleled sufferings of their ancestors who first settled in that ancient town, and for the erection of a suitable building for the accommodation of the meetings of said association."

Within four years, construction had started on a memorial hall. After the initial funds ran out, it took until 1834 before the building was completed.

Despite the society holding annual commemorative dinners, fundraising for the monument was difficult until 1850. At that time, the society resolved to erect a monument as well as a canopy over Plymouth Rock, and fundraising began to build momentum.

In 1856, sculptor Hammatt Billings agreed to build a small monument over the Rock within three years for an estimated $25,000, and a larger monument to the forefathers within 12 years at a cost of $300,000. As part of his agreement, Billing said he would coordinate the required fundraising and would protect the Pilgrim

Society against financial losses.

Over the next five years, the society reviewed a number of potential designs for the monument. The society originally planned to dedicate a monument near the harbor and Plymouth Rock until 1855, when the committee selected the design of the Billings monument.

The harbor site was considered too low and "too much surrounded with the more rude and ordinary scenes of life," so the monument was shifted from the harbor to the Allerton Street site, a location with a higher elevation.

Billings' original design for the monument called for it to be 150 feet high, with the Faith statue alone being 70 feet high. The monument's base was intended to have an interior chamber for displaying documents, as well as stairs to an observation deck on the platform supporting the Faith figure. The intent was for visitors to stand on the platform and view the harbor, Plymouth Rock and other sites associated with the

Pilgrims and the original settlement.

The cornerstones for the Forefathers Monument and the Plymouth Rock canopy were both laid on August 2, 1859. During the cornerstone ceremonies, an estimated 10,000 people poured into Plymouth and jammed the monument site.

The National Monument to the Forefathers under construction. Image was taken between 1878 (when Morality was dedicated) and 1888 (when Liberty was installed).

Fundraising for the rest of the monument was

delayed by the Civil War. After the war, inflation and cost considerations called for the monument's scale to be reduced before construction began in 1874. That year, Billings and the Pilgrim Society contracted with the Bodwell Granite Company of Vinalhaven, Maine, to build the pedestal (which was finished in late 1875).

Hammatt Billings died in 1874, and his brother Joseph took over fundraising and supervision of the monument project.

Joseph Billings and financial agent Willard M. Harding both died in 1880, bringing work on the monument to a halt. With funds low, the U.S. Government appropriated $15,000 for the Liberty statue and the Landing at Plymouth panel.

After the monument's completion in 1889, the Pilgrim Society purchased a home directly across Allerton Street to house a caretaker for the monument. The house was sold into private hands in 1992, and that property was subdivided in 2005.

Over the years, the site's view of Plymouth Harbor has largely been erased by extensive tree growth.

HAMMATT BILLINGS

The Forefathers monument was largely designed by noted Boston architect and illustrator Hammatt Billings. Born in 1818, Billings joined an architectural firm in 1837 and opened his own firm six years later.

Billings and his brother, Joseph, an engineer, collaborated on the design of the Boston Museum. The success of that commission established Billings' reputation, and led to engagements to design houses, churches, commercial buildings and libraries throughout New England.

In 1869, Billings was hired to design the campus of Wellesley College.

Billings was also a noted illustrator, and his most notable works include the first edition of *Uncle Tom's Cabin.*

Surprisingly little is known about Billing's personal life, other than financial problems that seemed to follow him through his career. More than once, he agreed to finance building projects that went over budget, causing financial strains that would be difficult to overcome.

Despite those problems, however, he remained a consistent and prolific architect and illustrator.

Billings' other notable works include the Civil War monument in Concord, Massachusetts, and he also designed the original granite canopy over Plymouth Rock.

Unfortunately, Billings died in 1874 at the age of 56, and did not live to see his design for the Forefathers Monument completed.

PLYMOUTH ROCK

Plymouth Rock (Boston Public Library)

One of the most famous symbols of early American history, Plymouth Rock has long been known as the site where the Pilgrims first landed in Plymouth.

Although none of the original settlers recorded their specific landing site, Plymouth Rock was identified as the location in 1741 by longtime resident Edwin Faunce, who was 95 at the time.

In 1774, as patriotic sentiments spread before onset of the American Revolution, Plymouth residents decided to move the rock from the waterfront to Town Hall. The rock broke, and only the top half was moved.

G 7327 Plymouth Rock, Plymouth, Mass.

The top section of the rock was later brought to the new Pilgrim Hall, and in 1867 it was returned to the waterfront and displayed under a protective canopy designed by Hammatt Billings.

As part of this project, the "1620" date was inscribed on the rock's surface.

The Billings canopy, finished in 1867, was 15 feet square and 30 feet high. Stone scallops atop the Plymouth Rock canopy represented "the pilgrim character of the enterprise of the Fathers," according to the 1863 edition of the "The Illustrated Pilgrim" almanac.

The monument featured four arches and iron railings to protect the rock from vandalism and the

theft of chips.

Once that canopy was replaced with its current structure in 1921, a number of artistic elements from the Billings canopy were incorporated into the Forefathers monument site.

ABOUT THE AUTHOR

Dave Pelland is also the author of *Civil War Monuments of Connecticut,* a guidebook to the state's 140 memorials to its Civil War veterans and heroes.